Narcissistic Rage: Understanding & Coping With Narcissistic Rage, Silent Treatment & Gaslighting

Lauren Kozlowski

Published by Escape The Narcissist, 2020.

While every precaution has been taken in the preparation of this book, the publisher assumes no responsibility for errors or omissions, or for damages resulting from the use of the information contained herein.

NARCISSISTIC RAGE: UNDERSTANDING & COPING WITH NARCISSISTIC RAGE, SILENT TREATMENT & GASLIGHTING

First edition. March 31, 2020.

Copyright © 2020 Lauren Kozlowski.

ISBN: 978-1393010074

Written by Lauren Kozlowski.

Table of Contents

Preface 1

What is Narcissistic Rage, and What Are the Triggers? 3

The Types of Narcissistic Rage 13

What Causes Narcissistic Rage? 19

'You Made Me Do It' - Or So The Narcissist Tells You 23

The Silent Treatment 31

How to Handle Silent Treatment 39

Gaslighting 45

The Temper Tantrums 55

Handling the Abuse: 6 Things to Remember to About Narcissism 59

Preface

The words 'narcissistic' and 'rage' are bad enough by themselves. When you merge them together, it becomes a force to be reckoned with; a volatile tornado that can emotionally destroy anything that dares enter its path. The term is as frightening and daunting as it sounds, and enduring the full force of narcissistic rage is enough to mentally and emotionally defeat just about anyone who gets in the way.

The actions and behaviors of the narcissist leading up to an episode of rage are just as anxiety-filled and hurtful as the rage itself. The walking on eggshells, the uncertainty of whether you're saying the right thing, the horrible feeling in your stomach when you sense you've done something wrong (but aren't certain what) are all emotionally crippling.

I know just how all of this feels; it was my entire life for such a long time. I was in a relationship with a malignant narcissist, so I have certainly had my fair share of narcissistic rage thrown my way. I know just how cruel, nasty, and abusive a narcissist can get when they get exposed or their 'true self' has been revealed. Narcissistic rage, which is sometimes called 'narcissistic injury', is a way to describe the way a narc behaves when they feel attacked. Narcissists have low self-esteem, believe it or not, so when they perceive something to reveal their insecurities or expose their insecure self, they lash out in the form of narcissistic rage.

What is Narcissistic Rage, and What Are the Triggers?

'Narcissistic rage' is a term that was first used in the psychology book 'The Analysis of the Self' which originally came out in the early seventies. In regard to terms used in psychoanalysis, 'narcissistic rage' is a pretty recent addition to the phrases used in the description of narcissistic traits. This rage is seen when the narcissist perceives that they are being attacked, in the most personal way, by you. As you may know, inflated self-worth, extreme vanity and an intense sense of entitlement are basic characteristics of this narcissistic personality disorder. So, when these traits are challenged or questioned by you, it will often lead to bouts of narcissistic rage.

Narcissistic rage is a direct reaction to narcissistic injury. This perceived 'injury' is a threat, from you to their sense of self; be it their self-worth or self-esteem. Their rages can be of two types, which I'll discuss a little more later on: explosive rage or passive-aggressive rage. The explosive types are just as they're described - monumentally explosive, often very scary, volatile outbursts which aren't always just verbal. They can often lead to violence and physical harm. In my case, I was subject to outbursts of violence, as well as a tirade of verbal humiliation and screaming. From speaking to other survivors of narcissistic abuse, I've come to understand the passive-aggressive type can be just as cutting and emotionally damaging. The passive-aggressive rages are shown in the form of withdrawal into moody, sulking, silent treatment as a means to punish and make the 'offender' pay for upsetting the narcissist.

If I dared to confront my abuser about their ill-treatment of me, their narcissistic rage was immediately unleashed on me. As I said before, a narc's self-esteem is very low (hence why they created this 'false self' to try to cloak their very insecure true self), so it often doesn't take too much to injure their frail sense of self. For example, one of my worst recollections of an episode of rage was when I pointed out to my ex that his timekeeping was bad. I didn't even do this in an accusatory way; I merely asked him if he was still picking me up from work at 5 pm, to which he replied 'yes'.

I half-jokingly replied that I should say I finish work at 4:30 pm, as that way he may be on time to pick me up. Time-keeping from my ex was very poor - he was often late or a no-show. My little joke was just a gentle way for me to remind my ex to be on time, as I often had to wait at least half an hour for him when he collected me from work. My ribbing didn't go down well at all; in stark contrast, an emotionally healthy person would see this jesting as a subtle way to say 'please don't be late again.' However, for a volatile and defensive narcissist, this was seen as a personal attack - a direct shot at one of their weak points, with the intent of hurting them.

As you can imagine, this perceived injury caused a huge bout of rage to erupt. His anger was uncontrollable. He began shouting at me, screaming insults and obscenities, accusing me of not appreciating him, of taking advantage of his 'good nature' (which was the opposite of the situation), and constantly 'nagging him'. These accusations were mixed with cursing, shoving, pushing, and *that* face he always pulled when I knew something bad was coming. The rage that filled inside of him spilled out onto his face, and I could see the anger in his eyes. Violence followed, and with my ex being a malignant narcissist, not much was off-limits. His rage knew almost no bounds.

In a passive-aggressive version of the same situation, the narc would go into themselves and punish you with their silent treatment or stone-cold sulking. They would make it so it's difficult to be around them, all the while making you feel as if it's your fault - that your actions brought on their upset reaction. Instead of taking on board the late joke, and understanding why it was said, the passive-aggressive narcissist would feel a sense of injustice that their ego was dented by you. As such, you will be made to pay in the form of silent treatment or cold one-word replies.

What differentiates narcissistic rage from healthy, normal anger is that it's usually highly unreasonable, disproportionate, and shockingly aggressive (or mind-bogglingly passive-aggressive). It's all because the narcs wants and perceived needs are not being met. It is a blow to their superficial, self-created self-image.

If you're unsure of how to detect narcissistic rage or are curious as to what the triggers of this are, I'll outline some below. This can help you differentiate narcissistic rage from normal anger.

Trigger 1: The narcissist doesn't get their own way, even when their request or want is unreasonable and/or unfair. For example, if you have the audacity to decline a request from the narcissist, such as sex, money, or if you refuse to do something for them, this will trigger their inner rage. How dare you say no to them! Don't you understand how in-demand, important, and superior the narcissist is?! There must be only one reason you've decided to decline their request: to upset them. For that, you'll see the darker side of the narcissist when they unleash their rage. If you dare refuse the narc what they want, they'll feel rejected, which is a big thing for them - rejection, to the narc, is pretty much affirming what they feel deep down: worthless and unimportant. For you to venture so close to an open wound will only result in a reaction of rage.

Trigger 2: The narcissist feels criticized, despite the critique being made constructively and reasonably. We're all human - we all get it wrong sometimes, we all make mistakes, and we all have to accept critique and feedback at times. Not a narcissist, however. 'Constructive critique' and 'feedback' equate to 'personal attack' and 'humiliation' to them. They, in their own version of themselves, are perfect. Any perceived imperfection is the fault of someone else, regardless of the lack of evidence to support this. Should you dare point something out to the narc that would chip away at their God-like perception of themselves, then you are seen as purposely trying to sabotage and humiliate the narcissist. Of course, rage will ensue if you need to broach a subject the narc needs to improve on. Naturally, this makes it difficult to talk to the narcissist about things that they're doing that are troubling you. Which, in true narc style, suits them perfectly.

Trigger 3: The narcissist isn't your center of attention, despite other things possibly needing to take priority. No matter if you're going through other things, or if you have stresses and worries outside of your relationship with the narcissist, the narcissist expects you to put them first. You have a sick mother? Your own health isn't so great? You have money issues? Your career has taken a nosedive?

The narcissist won't understand your heavy stress and concern for these things, and they don't expect those things to precede them in your attention. The narc has to be the most important thing in your life. I had many stresses in my life throughout my relationship with my abusive ex, and I went through these on my own. The narcissist, typically, isn't the supportive type, but moreover, they won't allow anything else to take over your attention. Should you put boundaries in place and let the narcissist know that you have other concerns right now, you'll be punished for that injury to them. In my case, as well as the verbal and physical assaults, my ex would use this time to behave as he wanted with the excuse 'you weren't giving me any attention', or 'I didn't think you cared because you weren't interested in me'.

So, when I was preoccupied with other life stresses, my ex would cheat on me. Should I find out, and expose him, he would gaslight me into believing that the issue was with me - that I had caused this due to not giving him enough attention. Of course, that's a ridiculous explanation, but you likely know yourself, a narcissist can make you believe pretty much anything when they have you in their grip.

Trigger 4: The narcissist has been caught out breaking rules or violating 'social norms'. By their very nature, narcissists don't take normal boundaries into consideration, so they very often overstep the mark with others. For example, myself and my ex were shopping in a very busy store. We had other errands to run after that one, and my ex was blatantly getting very agitated at the busyness of the shop we were in. Aside from taking it out on me and blaming me for 'coming shopping at such a stupid hour', he was getting very antisocial with the other shoppers around us when they wouldn't move out of the way immediately for him.

The final straw was when we were standing in line to pay, and the person before us didn't realize that it was his turn at the till. Instead of gently letting that person know they could go ahead and pay for their items like most people behind them in the queue would, my ex loudly huffed and marched ahead and jumped the line. Of course, this didn't go unnoticed by the person who should have been next at the till. They simply said, "Excuse me, I was next in line," to my ex. This enraged my ex, and he angrily retaliated to the innocent shopper. "How dare you speak to me with such disrespect!" my ex spat at the shocked man who dared to point out the fact that my ex was cutting the line.

Of course, this caused other shoppers to stop and watch this very awkward and unnecessary exchange between my ex and an innocent man who'd got caught off guard by narcissistic rage. My ex's sense of entitlement was challenged by this other man, so his go-to reaction was to lash out, despite the fact that he was in the wrong.

Trigger 5: The narc is asked by you to be accountable for their behavior(s). This is a huge one that will really get the narcs' rage to a boiling point. In fact, this is such a sensitive topic for most narcissists that their victims will only attempt this once or twice before knowing better than to question any bad or abusive behavior. All narcissistic rage points back to the injury they suffer at your hands, and when you pull them up on the horrible, nasty, hurtful being that they are, they don't want to hear it. It's not congruent with the person they want to be seen as, or as the person they see themselves as. Should you confront the narc with the person they really are, it's like unmasking them when they're ashamed of the face that's underneath. They'll try their best to pull the mask back over their insecurity and make you pay for daring to humiliate them like that.

Trigger 6: The narcissist suffers a blow to their egotistical sense of self by not being given 'special treatment' or being made the 'exception to the rule'. Being told 'no' is hurtful to a narcissist. It prods at their open wound of rejection. In order to make themselves feel important, they'll try to push their luck and be given exceptional treatment or perks that most others aren't given. This fuels their narcissistic ego, and helps (temporarily) close that open wound that fears rejection. Of course, life is full of 'no's' and closed doors; it's up to us to find workarounds or deal with the fact that no means no. To a narcissist, this is the ultimate disrespect. For example, my ex loved antiques, and buying and selling them was a hobby of his.

Part of this meant haggling with potential sellers to get the price lower. If a seller dared to reject my ex's offer, my ex would become enraged. He would feel disrespected, humiliated, berated, and belittled. Most of us in this situation would move on and seek opportunities elsewhere and forget about the perceived rejection. However, a narcissist will play this scenario over and over in their heads, raging at the audacity of someone telling them 'no'. The number of times my ex would come home and unleash his rage on me because he didn't get the deal he wanted, or because someone gave him an 'insulting offer' for one of his antiques was certainly in the double figures.

Trigger 7: The narc is reminded of their 'false-self' charade, their constant manipulation, their inner inadequacy, shame, and self-hatred. This trigger is seen when you, the recipient of the abuse, have become clued up to the game of the narcissist. Perhaps you've been reading up on it, listening to audiobooks, researching the topic to understand it (possibly what you're doing right now). However you've done it, you've come to understand the layers a narcissist has, and you know them for what they are now: a narcissist. You understand that their vile behavior stems from a place of self-loathing and insecurity, and you broach this realization with them. Whilst this may come from a place of understanding, compassion, and empathy, it won't be met with the same warmth as you expect. This, as with all triggers of narcissistic rage, comes from the humiliation and panic you've evoked within the narc, no matter how unwarranted those feelings are.

So, if you try to sit the narcissist down and talk through with them about their actions and how they display narcissistic tendencies, along with an outline of why they act the way they do, expect rage to follow. Whilst, deep down, the narcissist knows you're right, they can't confront that as the truth. They can't face their true self in the mirror, and by broaching this topic with them, you're essentially holding a mirror right up to them and forcing them to look. However, they won't let you get away with your exposing them, and the end result may even be you being accused of being the abusive narcissist.

Trigger 8: The narcissist fears they're not in control of their surroundings. Control is all for the narcissist. Controlling your actions, your thoughts of them, controlling their own self-image, controlling other people's ideas of them, controlling how other people act... 'control' and 'narcissism' go hand in hand. If the narcissist feels this control slipping, fear sets in, and rage comes spilling out. The narcissist likes to be the puppeteer, and for everyone else to be their puppets. If they sense that they can't control a situation, conversation, or event, they'll be off-kilter. They will be scared, full of fear that if they can't control something or someone, they'll panic that they're not as important, powerful, or special as they've tried to make out.

The above eight triggers may be things you've already experienced, but not managed to pinpoint as being 'narcissistic rage'. Of course, as humans, we all get angry now and again, and we (hopefully) do this in a healthy way and understand if we're being over-reactive or irrational. Often, we'll apologize if this is the case and hold our hands up to being in the wrong. It's important to know when normal anger becomes a narcissistic rage, so hopefully, the above triggers have helped you decipher the difference between the two.

The Types of Narcissistic Rage

I touched on this topic briefly earlier, but I'd like to give a bit more insight into the two types of narcissistic rage. There isn't a 'one size fits all' when it comes to describing narcissistic rage, because there are various types of narcissists. You have the covert, passive-aggressive narcissists that don't outright berate you and humiliate you, but they do it a very sneaky, subtle way. These types would rather allude to something and plant the seed in your brain, rather than blurting it right out. For example, instead of coming right out and telling you that you've put on weight, they'll say, "Are you sure you're comfortable in those jeans? They look a little tight,", or instead of telling you that you have no chance of securing that promotion at work, they'll say, 'Don't be disappointed with the outcome of your interview. You tried your best'.

Notice how the two passive-aggressive quotes there both tried to sound concerned or interested in the recipient's well-being; but also notice how hurtful and upsetting they are. Even if you act offended by the comments, a covert narcissist will simply deflect this by saying, 'I'm only looking out for you. You punish me for caring,' which is downright confusing to hear. The passive-aggressive narcissist is just as sneaky and quietly abusive with their form of narcissistic rage.

The passive type of narcissistic rage, whilst designed to ultimately punish you, does so much more: it's confusing, it's anxiety-filled, it feels like it lasts forever, and it focuses all of your thoughts and attention on the narcissist. Instead of outright telling you what you've done wrong, or what you've said to upset them, this type of narcissist will either make you guess what you've done (which is torture in itself), or you'll be subjected to the sulky silent treatment.

This silent treatment is pure emotional torture; you don't know how long the silence will last for, and the feeling of invisibility really affects your self-worth. No matter how many apologies you make to help speed up reconciliation, the timeframe that you have to endure the silent treatment is up to the narcissist. It's up to them how long you'll suffer for, and when you'll be free from this punishment.

I got talking to a woman whose ex-husband was a passive-aggressive narcissist, and she told me that if she somehow upset him or offended him, he would go for days and days without talking to her. He would go about his day as normal, and act like she wasn't there; he'd make his morning coffee (without making her one), he'd take his shower, iron his own gym gear (which his wife would usually do), prepare his lunch for work right beside his wife who was doing the same, all without saying a word to her.

He'd return home from work, and retire to the spare room where he'd remain until he repeated the process the next day. Whilst on the surface it sounds petty and childish, this narcissistic rage is actually very damaging and emotionally jilting. Throughout the sulks, silent treatment and being made to feel as if you don't exist, the narcissist is feeding off of your upset. They want to feel pined after. They want to have the powerful feeling of knowing they can hurt you without even saying a word. They want the ego boost of knowing as soon as they want to talk to you, you'll be there with open arms.

The woman who divulged her experience with a passive-aggressive narcissist to me explained just how it affected her ability to have a simple conversation with her husband at the time. Because she was so afraid of his reactions to being upset, and would never sit down and talk through any issues with her, she had to watch what she said to him. She couldn't bear having to go through the rigmarole of him shutting her out day after day, and her having to beg and plead with him to speak to her again.

The feeling of being exiled by the narcissist is something she says she's found hard to get over, and it affected her for a while after she got divorced from him. She really opened my eyes as to how affecting and upsetting this type of narcissistic rage is. I used to think that the word 'rage' didn't really apply to the passive-aggressive narc; before I committed to learning as much as I could about this topic, I wrote the passive-aggressive narcissist off as the 'easier' type of abuser, through my own ignorance. After discussing this topic with a number of survivors, I've come to understand just how equally debilitating this type of narcissist is. My own experiences have been with the type of narcissist who exhibited the explosive type of narcissistic rage. My ex was an over-the-top, larger than life, malignant narcissist, and his bouts of rage were cutting outbursts that were emotionally and often physically hurtful.

The explosive types don't beat around the bush. They don't 'allude' or 'suggest' things to you - they'll outright say what they think, and they don't sugar coat it. In fact, they do their best to avoid any sugar-coating whatsoever.

Should you upset a narcissist who is filled with explosive rage, you won't have to guess about what you've done to offend them or disgruntle them; they'll tell you, and they'll tell you exactly how stupid, worthless, cruel, crazy, insane, idiotic, and pointless you are. These types of narcissists react to injury with a heap of defensiveness, and they'll be sure to make you regret ever broaching the topic that made them erupt, or repeating the behavior that upset them.

As I said, this type of rage can be violent, but the violence isn't always just reserved for you. This type of narcissist is capable of hurting themselves, too. They might cut themselves, burn themselves, or inflict some sort of harm on themselves. From experience, and talking to others who've been through the same as me, this outburst of rage often occurs when you've confronted the narc about their behavior, and they feel backed into a corner. For example, if they've been messaging someone else and you've found the messages, or if they've been caught out lying and the proof you have is irrefutable, they take extreme measures to avoid confronting this truth.

This is a way for the narc to avoid having to answer for their despicable behavior, for you to be distracted by their self-harm, and for you to feel sorry for them enough to drop the subject moving forward. Instead of admitting their faults and expressing remorse, this type of narc will take to cutting themselves, harming themselves in some way or maybe just threatening to do so; either way, it's a distraction technique. On top of this, the abuser also often gets compassion and pity from their victim in this situation, which handily leads to the topic at hand getting buried and forgotten (in the narcissist's mind, anyway).

My ex, when I asked him for answers about his horrible treatment of me, or if I'd find evidence that he'd been lying or cheating, he would explode with his extreme bouts of rage. Often, his violence would be aimed at me or the surroundings. However, when I would confront him with something that he absolutely couldn't lie about, or worm his way out of, he would proceed to bang his head off the wall repeatedly. He would really go for it, too; he would smash his forehead and temple off our brick wall, leaving him badly bloodied and our white wall with stains of crimson.

Of course, this was a disturbing sight to see - he didn't just bang his head once or twice, he'd do it a dozen or so times, each time the sound of his skull hitting the wall making me sick to my stomach. This would always end with me patching him up, both of us crying, and him making empty threats to harm himself some more. To avoid this happening, I'd bury my need for answers to ensure my ex didn't do anything stupid to himself. Of course, this was the desired outcome for my ex: to avoid confrontation, to punish me for daring to question him, to gain my pity, and to ensure I wouldn't mention that topic again.

From the descriptions of the two types of narcissistic rage, you probably know what kind of narcissist you're dealing with, and you can probably see lots of parallels running alongside my descriptions and your own experiences. As I mentioned earlier, there isn't a 'one size fits all' description for a narcissist, but they are very predictable. They have similar behavioral patterns, similar phrases they use when they abuse you, and they all have similar reactions when confronted about their behavior; it just depends on what type of narcissist they are.

Now that I've covered the two types of rage, I'm going to move on to the three causes of narcissistic rage. These all boil down to the 'injury' the narcissist feels, but I'll explain each cause in a bit more depth to help you understand the narcs thinking process when it comes to perceived injury.

What Causes Narcissistic Rage?

I've used the term 'injury' quite a few times so far throughout this book, and I've touched on the triggers that cause the injury to manifest into narcissistic rage. However, I've not discussed what lies beneath the injury; the core reason the 'injury' is perceived as being such in the first place.

An emotionally healthy person can be offended and upset without retaliating with narcissistic rage. A mentally stable person would be able to talk about their offense, or more crucially, understand when there is no offense to be taken. So, what does the narcissist have within them that means their reaction to certain comments and situations is rage? What are their underlying feelings and thoughts that mean they feel the need to react so cruelly to often innocent comments or actions.

1. Their confidence has been challenged

A false appearance of self-confidence, self-assurance and unwavering entitlement are important traits to a narcissist. Underneath this appearance, however, is a person drowning in inadequacy and crippling insecurity. As you know, a narc often places unrealistic demands upon their spouse in the course of their relationship.

These tests are often a way for the narc to feel powerful, superior, and important; but, on occasion, these demands can also often lead to being challenged by their spouse - that being you. When challenged, the narc's extremely fragile ego can't accept the idea that they were wrong, questioned, or seen as being imperfect, which eventually leads to a seething loathing for the 'attacking' challenger. In the event of being questioned or challenged, the narcissist's red flags begin to go off: an attack being carried out upon them, and they must respond with sheer rage toward that person in order to regain the feeling of superiority they so desperately need.

1. They suffer injury to their esteem

Injury from a perceived attack to the narc's self-esteem triggers a resounding sense of shame and failure from their underlying sense of self issues. The narc projects their entitlement and abundance of self-importance to baffling extremes.

When a narcissist's failings or lack of real emotions are seen and then pointed out by others, the massive sense of shame overwhelms the narc, causing them to lash out at the 'attacker' or 'accuser'. Naturally, in true narc style, this feeling of injury overrides the narcissist's ability to react rationally and with a clear head. The all-consuming need for revenge, which is part of their explosive rage, doesn't die down until the narc has placed the desired amount of punishment upon the attacker. This, particularly with the malignant narcissist, can often lead to bouts of violence.

1. They fear their false sense of self has been exposed as fake

A narcissist has a false sense of who they are and also a false sense of their true capabilities and talents. Quite often, this falsehood is instilled into the narc during childhood. It's ingrained and nurtured by caregivers, who will accept nothing less than achievement from the child, putting pressure on the child to be perfect in their endeavors. Underneath that imagined sense of self is a narc who feels like they're not lovable for who they truly are, or what they can genuinely offer to a relationship. In a romantic relationship, when the narc thinks their spouse may be in disbelief or beginning to doubt who they really are, this causes their narcissistic rage to rise to the surface.

Narcissists are prone to getting involved in superficial relationships that only serve to nurture their false sense of self. When someone is seen as getting too close to the narcissist, this will disrupt the balance of who they want themselves to be with who their spouse actually perceives them to be, which only courts more defensiveness from the narcissist.

'You Made Me Do It' - Or So The Narcissist Tells You

Narcissistic rage doesn't come without a shed load of victim-blaming. The very nature of the rage is to deflect, demoralize and destroy, and blaming the victim is a sure-fire way to do this. The phrases, 'You make me act like this,' or 'You know when you do that, what will happen,' still make me wince. These deflective, blame-shifting words do a ton of damage to a dumbfounded, confused victim who will often end up taking the misplaced blame and accept it as the truth.

Looking back, I would wonder why I accepted such abhorrent and blameful treatment. When I sought out answers for this, I traced it back to my childhood. My mother was a tough parent, and I was rarely given empathy or even the basic comfort a growing child needs. If I spilled my drink at the table, she would yell and scream, despite it clearly being an accident. She'd call me stupid, clumsy, and blame me for the mess around the house. If I had fallen over and grazed my knees, she'd coldly tend to my wounds whilst reminding me that I was to blame for making her late for an appointment. I didn't really know what it felt like to be shown comfort or empathy, although I had it in abundance to give.

A lot of the negative things in her life weren't her fault - they were mine. Her career hadn't advanced as much as it should have, because she had to take care of me. Her social life was dead because I wasn't responsible enough to be left alone whilst she went out. She was in debt because she had to look after me. So, from a young age, I understood that I was to blame for many things, and I believed this to be true. It was only after I entered (and subsequently escaped from) a narcissistic relationship did I realize that my mother had instilled into me an inner acceptance of blame.

I'm not saying this is the root cause for every victim of narcissism to accept the blame they are dished out, but I think it's important to look back to different episodes of your life to see where certain things took root. Only then can we work to fix these internal dents and wounds that leave us open to such horrible treatment.

I'd like to go over the five techniques a narcissist uses to shift blame back to the victim to make you more aware of when this may be happening to you. If this is happening to you, regardless of how you react externally to the narcissist, I want you to know that, in reality, you're not to blame. No, you didn't make the narcissist do it, you're not to blame for the narcs past, nor are you at fault for anyone who may have ill-treated them in the past.

Blame Tactic 1: Playing victim

This is undeniably one of the most common victim-blaming techniques. In this situation, you may ask your other half to stop criticizing, mocking, belittling or ridiculing you... no matter what the specific scenario, you're asking your spouse to stop a behavior or action that you find upsetting and hurtful. Since this paints you as the victim, the narc is super quick to turn the tables on you, because they can't have you openly being a victim - they have to be more of a victim than you. Instead of listening to your legitimate concerns and requests for empathy, they will bring up (or, sometimes, simply make up) something that is often totally unrelated from the past in which they claim that you've hurt them. Quick as a flash, the emotional tables have turned, and you're the one saying sorry to them.

This is something my ex was highly skilled in doing. No matter how hurt I would tell him he was making me, how much his words hurt me, or how upset his actions were causing me to become, he would never accept accountability. Instead, he would retort with, 'What about the time you did this,' or 'I think you're forgetting when you did that,' which served to a) stop me from being the victim, b) divert my pleading for empathy onto something that revolved around his feelings and c) gain some narcissistic supply from my pity, empathy and compassion towards him and his upset.

Blame Tactic 2: Minimizing your feelings

If the narc hurts your feelings, you certainly have every right to calmly let them know that and to ask them to stop. Often, this can lead to them laughing at, dismissing, or ridiculing your hurt feelings. Your hurt will be further humiliated by the use of phrases like, 'You're way too sensitive,' or, 'You're totally crazy... you have no sense of humor,' or, 'You're hysterical. You need to seriously calm down!'

The blame is then no longer on the narc for their treatment of you, but instead, it's now on you for reaction to their abhorrent treatment of you. It's a frustrating irony that if you ever criticize a narc, the same way that they criticize you, they turn to narcissistic rage. Looking back, it's borderline laughable that they have the front to act like this and blame you for having such fragile emotions. It's an irony that only becomes apparent after you've left the relationship usually.

Blame Tactic 3: Arguing about the arguing

Each argument becomes a debate about the argument itself, instead of the initial point you were trying to get across. They lure you into these fruitless fights, changing the intention of their words and debating logic simply in order to put you on the defensive. Instead of talking through your legitimate points or concerns, they'll comment on your tone, the language you're using, the intent behind your words and they'll accuse you of doing things they're doing. Cleverly, the narc has now ensured that the blame is no longer on them, but now the argument is focused on the way you broached the argument in the first place.

Again, this deflection tactic is frustrating and crazy-making. It strips you of the ability to have your voice heard, and it serves to muffle your cries for some understanding.

Blame Tactic 4: Guilt tripping and tales of pity

As someone who has become involved with a narcissist, it's very likely that you're prone to feeling sympathetic to others, have an abundance of empathy, and really feel for those who have been through hard times in life. Those traits are brilliant characteristics that a narcissist will look for in a partner because they can exploit them. It's those same traits that will supply them with a lot of ego-boosting and will offer them a sympathetic ear to listen to their stories of woe. Because of this, it's likely that the narc will pull this manipulation tactic out of the bag quite a lot.

If you mention something hurtful they've done, they'll then divert to talking about their abusive childhood or an ex that utterly wronged them and destroyed them - whatever their go-to story is, they'll pull it out of their arsenal to stop you in your tracks. Again, before you have time to comprehend just what's going on, you're the one comforting them, even though they were the one who was being called out on their bad behavior. The manipulative narcissist is banking on your empathetic and understanding nature for this one; how can you possibly be mad at someone who's so hurt, especially when they open up to you about it?

We all go through heartache, hard times, trials and tribulations in life. But emotionally healthy people don't even consider using those bad experiences as excuses to hurt and upset others, and they don't bring up those sad tales and stories of pity to (often conveniently) avoid accepting accountability for their behavior.

My ex had a rough childhood. His dad disciplined him harshly, and his mother died when he was a teenager. If I pulled my ex up on his poor treatment of me, sometimes his response would be to use his bad life experiences to excuse his behavior. If he got aggressive? It was because his dad showed him *that* was how to deal with emotions. If he cheated? It's because his mother wasn't around to show him how to treat women.

Blame Tactic 5: The last resort

The last resort is usually utilized when they've been quite blatantly caught red-handed or called out for something they can't deny they did wrong. Shame isn't an acceptable feeling to people with a narcissistic personality disorder, so even though some of their last resort excuses are laughable, they are there to stop the narc feeling the degrading feeling of being in the wrong. So they'll throw you an unfounded, terribly awful accusation.

You thought this was an open and shut case. You have an abundance of proof, the clearly incriminating evidence, everything you need to rightfully call the narc out for their horrid behavior. You think there is no way they can come back with anything but the truth. And, to your utter disbelief, then they come back with a complete curveball. It's a nonsensical reply, often untrue and usually full of shocking allegations. It can be something like:

You abuse me.

You're violent towards me.

I know you've cheated on me.

You're deranged - you're mentally ill.

You've never, ever loved me.

You're obsessive, you stalk me, you scare me.

That open and shut case you thought you had isn't so clear anymore. Now you're defending yourself against wild allegations that you never could have even imagined carrying out. There's no way you could ever prepare for this level of craziness, and this is what the narcissist is banking on.

The Silent Treatment

Words can cut like a knife. But so can silence.

This unseen and unheard form of abuse is so frustratingly hurtful because it's hard to verbalize. It almost sounds childish to say, 'I'm upset because my partner isn't speaking to me'. I remember trying to tell a friend at the time just how hurt I was as my ex had ignored me for two days straight after I referred to the places we lived as 'my house' instead of 'our house'. It was an innocent slip of the tongue, but my ex took it as an insult. He said I called it 'my house' because I was paying the majority of the bills at the time, and I wanted to remind him that I was the breadwinner. He said I was trying to humiliate him in front of others, which I know wasn't the case; it was simply an innocent comment. But, he ignored me for days after this to punish me for my incorrect wording.

When I tried to talk about my upset with my friend at the time, she said I was being silly and that I should take advantage of this time and 'enjoy the peace'. She clearly didn't understand or comprehend just how hurtful his silent treatment was. I was in bits. I didn't know how long the silent treatment would last, or how long I would be made to feel invisible for. I wanted to find some comfort from my friend, for her to empathize and perhaps offer me some words of advice. Instead, she acted like I was being childish, and she almost reinforced to me that my ex's treatment of me was okay. It was at this point that I looked for some answers on silent treatment, and I read blogs, articles and books on the subject which lead me to a deeper understanding of the term 'narcissistic abuse'. From here, I found out as much as I could about silent treatment, which guided me to the term 'narcissistic rage'. Silent treatment and rage went together like bread and butter. Whilst the words 'silent' and 'rage' seem like they'd be total opposites, they merge together to become a deadly weapon in the narc's arsenal.

I believe that silent treatment is one of the cruelest and without a doubt one of the most heartbreaking abuse tactics the narc uses. I recall when my dog ate something he shouldn't have (which was poisonous to him), how utterly devastated I was. My dog was kept in the vets for a few days, and we were unsure as to what was going to happen. They'd managed to pump his stomach, but he wasn't getting any better. The vets told me the next day or so was critical, and for that time I was in pieces. Some friends gave me support, but throughout the whole episode, my ex was as cold as ice. He offered me no comfort, empathy, or understanding. In fact, all he offered me was his stone-cold silence.

He completely pulled away from me, acting like I didn't even exist. He'd done this before in a time of need, but I found this especially challenging, as I'd really done nothing wrong. The pain of me, as a dog lover, not knowing if my dog would be coming back from the vets, coupled with him shutting me out, made it unbearable.

Eventually, he broke his painful silence by attacking me relentlessly about how everyone else that I had sought comfort from was more important to me than he was. He brought up how disgusting and manipulative I was to use the illness of my pet as a way to get attention and sympathy from others. Of course, this is him projecting, but at the time I felt totally beside myself.

If he heard me crying, or if he overheard me sobbing in the bathroom alone, he would momentarily break his silence to let out a disbelieving laugh, or a fed-up sigh.

Now that I can understand how narcissists work, I know this complete emotional abandonment from my ex transpired because of his narcissistic rage, which came about when I wasn't as available to him to provide narcissistic supply. When I was concerned about my dog, the attention wasn't solely on him, which he despised. What he hated just as much was the comfort and sympathy other people were giving me.

I think it's probable that you have suffered at a narcissist's hands like this when you've been in need, and they have most likely abandoned and ignored your needs, and in some circumstances, perhaps even cut off all contact with you. This could even mean things as serious and heartbreaking as family deaths or terminal illnesses.

If you become too emotionally 'high maintenance' for the narc, and wind up needing their support (heaven forbid), a narcissist is then more likely to begin their hunt for a fresher source of narcissistic supply who will fluff their ego and feed their falsified self. A friend of mine was good friends with a lady who was in palliative care after being diagnosed with a rare form of cancer. It shocked and saddened me to hear that, whilst bedridden, this lady's husband had put himself on dating sites and was meeting future spouses to prepare for his wife's imminent death. This, to me, screamed of a narcissist who was in full throttle with his rage: almost like *how dare my wife die and leave me alone?*

He couldn't even contain himself until she had passed away. To him, it was totally justifiable - 'but what about me' was his argument for his behavior.

With this in mind, I'd like to talk more about how narcs use silent treatment in order to get new sources of supply.

I recently met up with an old friend whose narcissistic spouse would very frequently go quiet and withdraw from her. Subsequently, he would disappear, without warning or even anything to hint that he was going to vanish. He would be completely uncontactable throughout the entire time he disappeared, which would vary from weeks at a time to months on end. Eventually, but not totally surprisingly, she discovered that he was, in fact, spending time with other women during these vanishing acts.

Usually, when narcs go MIA, they're often up to no good. To the narc, it's such a relief to escape the perceived confinement of being 'average'. This feeling of mediocrity is not congruent with their false self. The thought of being average makes them race to feed their false idea of who they are, so they'll seek significance from fresh supply and new excitement.

So, if a narc has pulled away and is ignoring you, there's every chance that they are seeking a new supply. As hurtful as that may be to hear, I honestly can't think of one single example of someone telling me about the silent treatment they endured and the sudden disappearances they were put through where this wasn't eventually outed as the truth. If things aren't going great with the newest source of supply, the narc may jump ship and return to you. The narc will break their silence, begin communicating with you, but will offer very little of an explanation for their actions. They'll expect to pick it up with you exactly where they left it.

The victim who has endured all of this will usually avoid interrogating the narc and reconnect without much of a fight, just so they can get some (temporary) relief from the unbearable emotional trauma they're feeling. In some cases, the victim may feel powerless not to reconcile, and the abusive cycle continues, stripping away their self-worth more and more each time it comes full circle.

The friend I was speaking to, whose spouse would vanish sporadically, told me that she would offer him more of herself when he eventually returned each time. This was in a futile attempt to get him to stay, and not return to his adulterous ways. But it happened again and again until he eventually left her for good, for another woman. This time, the silent treatment had led to the final discard.

Lots of victims, when enduring silent treatment, will panic as their fears of abandonment surface intensely. Years ago, I was one of these people. I would track my abuser down and beg him to come back. At the same time, I would give in to his outrageous demands and feel I had no choice other than to accept full responsibility for whatever he accused me of doing to provoke his silent treatment. Even though I knew deep down, I hadn't done what he was accusing me of, I did this to keep him in my life.

Eventually, when I found my strength and silent treatment no longer worked on me, this is when my ex began his 'hoovering' tactic. This is what makes the abuse come full circle; dropping you like trash, hoovering you up, only to drop you like trash again. Hoovering was especially utilized by my ex when it appeared I was getting on with life without him. I would no longer attempt contact, and this would be when he would reappear in my life. As you can imagine, nothing was ever resolved, and the seemingly endless cycle of abuse was what my life had turned into. The untended traumas that kept me stuck in this loop were playing out over and over.

That was the case until I set my boundaries and went no contact for the umpteenth and final time. It was only when I resolved to make this time the one where I was going to cut all ties and move on for good that I could heal. I've had people say to me, 'going no contact is just running away from your problems, and makes you no different to the narcissist. They give you the silent treatment, so you go no contact? It sounds childish.' When someone said this to me, my initial reaction was anger. How dare they minimize the boundaries we need to put in place to protect ourselves? However, to someone like this, the best thing to do is explain the rationale for going no contact.

No contact is, in reality, a healthy technique that is necessary if we want to save ourselves, rebuild our life and give our soul the much-needed healing it deserves. This isn't some vengeful tactic used to degrade and punish someone for their actions. It's a bold statement of 'I'm going to start taking care of me and say *no more* to the abuse I'm enduring'.

In stark comparison, narcissistic silent treatment carries a very different message. It says to the victim, 'you're worthless, you don't deserve my time, you're not worthy of having me in your life'.

Permanent silent treatment from the narc happens because the narcissist has changed their stage or 'film set'. The people who are no longer relevant to the fictitious, pathological requirements of the narc's false self are discarded.

This hurts, without a doubt. Whilst it's a blessing in disguise, you can't see this at the time. You feel utterly heartbroken and abandoned. But you must use this space and silence to your advantage. During this time, you have to detach, make a serious effort to pull away and remove yourself from this toxic soul-sucking person. This mentality, coupled with the time you have to process everything you've endured, allows you to heal. By doing this, you allow yourself to be able to live life on your terms, find a deserving love and become everything you are truly capable of.

When you endure narcissistic abuse, you suffer severe emotional trauma–you become depressed, emotionally drained, and mentally broken. You live in a state of confusion, unworthiness, and anxiety. None of this is eased by the narcissist - there is no true comfort or healing to be found there.

Take this opportunity to do the most important task of your life this far, which is to completely detach from the narc, withdraw all of your attention away from them, and look inwards to heal the traumatized and broken parts of you that the narc has so purposefully tried to destroy.

How to Handle Silent Treatment

It may seem like an unachievable mean feat, but you can shut down the narc during episodes of silent treatment. The narcissist wants you to feel like they hold the power, and you're entirely unable to do anything about it. Their presence, or often lack of, can demolish you into little pieces, and make you feel like your heart has been ripped from your chest. Of course, the narcissist knows this; they relish in it.

In times like this, when you feel utterly helpless and desperate, feeling so devoid of any hope that you can stand up to this type of vile mistreatment from the narc. Nothing except the narcissist themselves can make you feel 'normal' again. You just yearn for them to speak to you, to care enough to be with you, and for them to stop with their dehumanizing silent treatment. These downtrodden emotions override the desire to overcome this abuse and disarm the narc of their ability to make you feel so traumatized. You feel like there is only one way out of the painful pit that you're in: back in the arms of the narcissist.

This isn't true.

I want to show you how to shut down the narcissist during their next episode of silent treatment. I want to give you the mindset to know how to walk away with your dignity intact, feeling empowered with your ability to stop the silent treatment from destroying you.

Disarming the Narcissist During Episodes of Silent Treatment

#1 – First of all, don't believe for one more second it's your fault.

This one is so, so important. I've placed it first on this list because it lays the solid mental foundation you need to disarm the narc when they put you through these episodes of silence.

I know just as much as you that when we get the dreaded silent treatment from the narc in our life, it is utterly crippling. Even if we know, deep down, that the abuser is in the wrong, we take on the burden of responsibility for their devastating silence.

This is what the narcissist wants.

Let me give you a 'healthy' comparison: normally, when upset or after an argument, people may need some time alone to think and digest how they feel, but they don't ever use the silent treatment as a way to punish their spouse. After some healthy thinking time, most couples will reconcile, admit their shortcomings, and work on a resolution together. Despite things perhaps getting heated, and feelings can be intense after an argument, healthy couples don't need to worry about their other half punishing them or ignoring them or disappearing on them.

Someone who truly cares about you, and their relationship with you, will come back and want to have a conversation about how to improve things moving forward. If someone really cares about you, they won't try to make you feel like it's all your fault because they did something hurtful or deceitful.

When someone is a narcissistic abuser, their aim isn't to work things out. Rather, it's to work out how they can maintain their power and sheer control over you and the relationship as a whole. So, when you go days and days without receiving any communication from them, keep this in mind.

#2–Make a serious effort to disengage - slowly you will find this gives you more power.

The very last thing you want to do during an episode of silent treatment is to fuel the narcissist by engaging with them when they (invariably) try to hoover you.

For those of you just learning about what hoovering is, I'll give you a quick description: Hoovering is a manipulation tactic employed by narcs to lure their victims back into a relationship with them by showing falsified improved and desirable behavior. It's aptly named after the vacuum cleaner because the narcissist sucks you back in like a Hoover. It's also gained this name because, ultimately, you'll be treated like dirt.

Hoovers don't just occur after a discard, though. In reality, most discards aren't even genuine. When the narc apparently discards you, it's more often than not all smoke and mirrors to trigger your abandonment fears. This benefits the narcissist because they predict you'll accept their horrible behaviors and eventually give in to them just to have them in your life.

When the narcissist finally tries to communicate during silent treatment, you don't want to fluff up their smug sense of entitlement by responding to them. I know that often our go-to emotions are empathy and guilt, and we try to understand why they disappeared on us.

Here's some tough love: this way of thinking will make sure you're a victim for as long as you retain the pandering mindset you have towards the narc. I did it for so long, I want to make sure that no-one else is trapped by the mindset the narcissist has instilled into them. With narcissists, you want to show them that their actions are not right in any way at all. When they eventually do reach out after the silent treatment, you should make sure they are met with complete indifference.

Ideally, their attempt to connect should be met with silence, but I know this can take some working up to. Whilst you work up to having the strength to know you shouldn't respond to them, being indifferent and not caving in to their manipulative ways will help you build up to becoming emotionally tough enough to say, 'enough is enough'. The more you do this, the more the narc begins to recognize that their manipulative game didn't work this time. This gives you power.

#3–Turn the silent treatment into your victory song.

As I mentioned, I know it takes some mustering up to before going no-contact, but trust me when I say, the best way to shut down a narcissist who is giving you the silent treatment is to use the opportunity to end the relationship. Block them, delete them, and shut them out from being able to contact you.

This is what I eventually did after receiving the silent treatment for the umpteenth time. I used it as an opportunity. I took the hurt and turned it into something I could capitalize on. Of course, this requires a lot of discipline, and you need to obtain a certain mindset before you can make it work this way.

In your head, you let go of the seemingly solid belief that you need to be with the narcissist in order to feel good. You need to let go of the false thinking that, if you don't have the narc with you, you'll never find someone like that again - even if this is something they take glee in telling you (much like my ex).

You need to cultivate a frame of mind where you accept there will be a hard road ahead of you, but it's a path you need to be willing to go down in order to get to a place of healing. When you're healed, and you're YOU again, you make space for a loving, entirely reciprocal relationship when the time is right. Let go of the endless waiting for apologies and the fruitless wait for closure from the narcissist.

Gaslighting

The word 'rage' has you imagining monumental fits of anger, aggressive outbursts, and prolonged periods of hostility, which can certainly describe symptoms of narcissistic rage. However, as I mentioned, this isn't the only way a narcissist can exhibit rage. Narcs are undoubtedly clever, but they tend to not use that intelligence for anything other than their own selfish requirements and manipulative ways.

Narcissists, particularly when you've escaped a relationship with one and can look back at it in hindsight, are quite predictable.

This idea was solidified when I began connecting with other survivors of narcissism and we shared our stories of abuse with one another. We noticed and agreed that our former spouses would act in the same way, exhibit the same child-like behavior, and have almost identical put-downs, manipulative phrases, and criticisms. It became quite humorous - we would be recounting the abusive things our exes had said to us, and we found we were able to finish the end of each other's sentences before they were said - all because we'd heard those put-downs so many times before!

Whilst it was a surreal way to bond with other survivors, it also gave me some solace that the manipulative phrases I heard weren't true - so many other survivors have had to hear the same cutting and hurtful phrases as me. It was a bittersweet realization because for far too long, I'd bought into and believed all of the things my ex had said to me. His gaslighting was first-class, and he was so good at it, I didn't even realize it was happening. Even for a while after the relationship ended, I was still learning the extent to which I had been manipulated, and I was shocked at just how naïve (or so I felt) I had been.

This chapter, dedicated to the mind-fogging mental abuse of gaslighting, aims to outline just how covertly the narc can abuse you, and show you how seemingly innocent (yet very hurtful) comments are part of their abusive cycle.

Particularly for a covert narcissist, beneath their quieter nature and apparent sensitive front, lurks a person filled with contempt and a bulging sense of entitlement. Their manipulative tactics work to completely diminish, demean and ruin their victims behind closed doors–which goes a long way to explain how their manipulation and sheer exploitation can leave their victims blindsided and emotionally stumbling from the unexpected psychological attacks they are being subjected to.

To discuss this further, I'm going to talk about the three manipulation techniques that primarily covert narcissists use. The tips included on how to handle it if you encounter one are provided by the many survivors of covert abuse that I've spoken to. Whilst they want to remain anonymous, they also want to help educate others and were keen for me to use their experiences and advice to give this chapter the best perspective possible. Whilst I'm a victim of a malignant narcissist, I do still recognize some of the sneaky abuse I'll outline below; it's not just confined to the abuse received at the hands of a covert narcissist, but merely more likely to be given at the hands of a covert type abuser.

Gaslighting Technique #1: Confusing double meanings, mind-fogging put-downs and the use of coded language.

A mind-fogging put-down occurs when a narcissist is threatened by somebody else's intelligence, status, abilities, looks or any other resources they may be envious of. It involves hurling their victim off their pedestal, whilst at the same time, offering them some hope for getting back on it. So that the narcissist can put their victims down but still evade having to take accountability, the narc will initially offer a nice compliment, followed by a cutting takedown. For example, 'You've done a really good job of losing weight! Too bad it's fallen off in all the wrong places, eh?' This was a direct quote from my ex. Yes, he was congratulating me on my weight loss - but he also implied I looked worse despite all of my hard work.

This can also work the opposite way around–the narc may begin their sneaky attack with a highly critical opening, only to go ahead and soften (the use of the word 'soften' is loose here) the harsh blow with a lowly crumb of a compliment to engender confusion in the victim. Another quote from my ex: 'The job you're in is very basic. You could train a monkey to do it! Ah, well at least you work hard.' Simultaneously berating me for a job he felt wasn't good enough, let bread crumbing me with a 'hardworking' compliment. This serves to make their put-down appear more like a genuine, constructive critique rather than a ploy to demolish your spirit. It conditions the victim, with frequent use over time, to forever be seeking the narc's approval and backing.

Manipulative narcissists will send a fog-inducing mixed message by contradicting their seemingly harmless words with a malicious undercurrent. This may include giving you a compliment with a patronizing tone of voice, telling a 'joke' at your expense with a taunting look. It can also be seen by the narc using a certain gesture or maddening facial expression or by saying something that can very easily have two meanings (one is always more innocent, and the other, offensive, hurtful and downright abusive). As always, the narc will try - often succeeding - to convince you that they never intended to for the abusive meaning to come across that way, but the victim always senses the undercurrent of something more sinister in such an interaction.

They may also engage in a sort of 'coded' or 'secret' language. This can mean putting you down in the company of others by making fun of something that they full-well know you're sensitive about, but the others around may not know that it's a vulnerability of yours. Like an inside joke, but simply aimed at you in order to deliver as much hurt and humiliation as possible. It also intends to evoke a response from you that may seem over the top or excessive to others looking in, who aren't part of this 'inside joke'. This is a very sneaky way for the narcissist to get away with their abhorrent abuse and provoke their victim to react in front of an audience. They will then use their victim's reactions as a form of proof when convincing others that their spouse is 'unhinged', 'overly emotional' or a 'psycho'.

NARCISSISTIC RAGE: UNDERSTANDING & COPING WITH NARCISSISTIC RAGE, SILENT TREATMENT & GASLIGHTING

Gaslighting often starts with a series of very subtle mind games that intentionally prays on the victim's limited ability to tolerate uncertainty or instability in the relationship. This is done, in a very cerebral and calculating way, to damage the victim's understanding of their own reality and their sense of self. When the victim is confused and left thinking, 'What's going on?', there is often a reluctance to see the abuser for who they really are. It's this abuser-instilled denial that is the backbone of a narcissistic relationship.

The victim reduces their own cognitive dissonance and not being able to understand the situation by instead 'believing' in their abuser's recollection of events. Eventually, these covert humiliations, secret messages, and double-sided comments become part of a warped version of reality that the manipulator has built.

Advice: When encountering this kind of gaslighting, avoid reacting to the hypercriticism and cutting words as much as possible. Where possible, leave the conversation as soon as possible. The more emotionally responsive you are to the gaslighting, the more the narc will mentally note that information and proceed to use that exact tactic again in the future, simply to provoke you. If you show emotion to their hurtful words and secret language in front of others, understand that they will use your reactions as 'verification' that you're unstable. As much as you possibly can, keep your cool.

If you are unsure as to whether you've endured gaslighting, a good way to ascertain this is to compare the way your spouse has reacted to your successes and accomplishments to the way other (emotionally healthier) people you know have. I'll predict that the healthier people in your life will have celebrated you and congratulated your achievement whereas the narcissist would find negative points and ways to put you down.

Gaslighting Technique #2: Diversion.

To distract you from the fact that they're gaslighting you, the narc will create all sorts of wild diversions to prevent you from staying logical and grounded in your own knowledge of what has just happened. This is so they can disguise their malicious want to take full control and power over you and the relationship by ensuring that you're always in a frightened state of walking on eggshells. Instead of picking up on and calling them out on their abusive ways, the narc instead gets you to look at your own fabricated misgivings and flaws.

One second, they may be making a horrid comment about the way you look, and the next, they're being sickly sweet and complimentary about how perfect you are, as well as how you 'read too much into what they say' when you show your utter confusion about their seemingly sudden switch of persona. Later, they'll plan a special date night with you, then all of a sudden, they're berating you for daring to expect that of them in the first instance, despite the fact that it was their idea to do so in the first place. By unpredictably switching from utter pain to confusing pleasure, from unhappiness to absolute admiration, the narc is able to hide the fact that they're battering you emotionally, with great intent.

This is how they can divert from the truth that they're manipulating you and purposefully setting you up for absolute failure: by frequently shifting the goalposts. Notice how they swiftly change the subject when they feel like you're broaching their bad behavior. Sentences like, 'I'm not wasting my time trying to make you see the truth,' can be common when the narc is called out on their manipulative ways. No matter what you do, the narcissist will hardly ever be satisfied with you.

Advice: As best as you possibly can, stay true to what you experienced. I know this can be hard when faced with a serial manipulator, but ground yourself with the understanding that you're being subjected to gaslighting. Observe the ongoing patterns of the behavior you're being subjected to and marry it up against what the narc claims to be doing (or not doing as the case may be). A narcissist's predatory behavior will tell you a whole lot more than their manipulative, contradictory words ever can. When a narcissist tries to steer you away from a topic by pointing out something unrelated, you did or said or tries to completely end the conversation before it's begun, repeat the facts, maintain your true understanding of the issue and end the interaction; don't give in to their gaslighting.

Gaslighting Tactic #3. Minimization.

This is when the narcissist becomes hyper-focused on something irrelevant to minimize something you've done, achieved, accomplished, or are happy about. For example, if you've recently got a promotion at work, the narcissist might start asking about when you plan to get a job in upper-management. If you've just signed the lease on an apartment you've spent years dreaming of, they might divert the subject to being about something in your neighborhood being 'unsavory'. For a gaslighting narcissist, they will always find a way to crawl inside of your head.

The appearance of minimization can help you in identifying who the narcissist actually is in a group; whilst others would be outwardly congratulating you on a good job, the narc is often somewhere in the background, avoiding the fuss being made over you. They're likely alone and sulking, ready to burst your happy bubble. They will gladly be the harsh needle to your proud balloon with a backhanded dig, plenty of critiques or an obnoxious comment about something they think you're lacking in.

When a narcissist makes you feel insecure, unsure and unbalanced, it's very frequently because they don't want to face their own deep-seated emotional issues and the horrible realization that they may not be as special as they really want to believe.

Advice: Resist the minimization by maximizing your own self-approval. Rather than focusing on the narc's jealous attempts to degrade and minimize you, adjust your focus to the people who are truly celebrating you and your accomplishments.

Understand that the narcissist's minimization is a hidden confession of their envy of you. You, simply by being you, are threatening their false sense of superiority; this just shows how fragile a narcissist is.

Don't forget to celebrate yourself, too. Self-validation is one of the most powerful weapons you can have when fighting against the relentless sabotage of a narcissist.

The Temper Tantrums

The rage-filled outburst of a narcissist is like a two-year-old having one of their temper tantrums. It comes out of nowhere, creates an often embarrassing and unnecessary scene, and is served to shock others into behaving in a way the narc wants. It's hugely selfish behavior, and everything suddenly becomes about them and what they need or want. Just like a toddler, a narc seemingly can't tell the difference between what they need and what they desire. The two things, to a narcissist, are exactly the same and as such their rage is sparked by both if they don't get what they're craving.

This brief chapter is going to talk about these temper tantrums; they're not quite a full-blown rage, but it's still hugely affecting and upsetting to endure, and can often lead to episodes of full-on narcissistic rage.

So what brings on these horrible, humiliating tantrums? Why does the narcissist seem to be wired like a toddler, to not understand the basic adult knowledge of being able to tell the difference between need and want?

There are five reasons that a narc will reveal their inner toddler and have a tantrum, and I'll outline them here:

#1 - Their fantasy has been shattered

Toddlers think imaginary, they don't think logically. Narcs also have the ignorance to live in their own imaginary, self-created word. However, the world carved out by a narcissist is much less innocent and cute than the one a toddler with conjure up. The narcissist's distorted perception of reality sees them as being powerful, often more beautiful than they really are, all-knowing, highly authoritative, and always right. Should that imaginary world be shattered, it's met with immediate, rageful anger.

Just like telling a child that Santa isn't real, or the tooth fairy no longer brings them money because it never existed, this reality is met with denial, defiance, and anger. If you dare to hold the mirror of reality up to a narcissist, a narcissistic tantrum is to be expected.

#2 - Their insecurity has been found out

At the core of every narc, is deep-seated insecurity that causes them a great deal of shame or doubt - things like abuse, a poor childhood, or not being a high achiever. Most of the displayed 'I'm better than you' actions exhibited by the narc is in an effort to cover up that painful insecurity they work so hard to conceal. But as soon as it's revealed, the narcissist becomes rageful and angry in order to deflect their (perceived as being) shameful image.

#3 - Disputing their superiority

Narcissists view themselves as being highly superior to others in most aspects, including intelligence, social status, and influence. Any perceived challenge to that image they have of themselves is met with quick retaliation and defensive reactions. They must be on top at all costs, even if it means forfeiting their integrity, honesty and treating others with respect.

Should you throw their 'better than everyone' persona into question, and doubt their facade, they'll throw one of their toddler-like temper tantrums.

#4 - Needing to be the center of attention

Exactly like a two-year-old, some narcs (particularly the malignant kind in my experience, but not just limited to that type) have discovered that if they can't get positive attention, then negative will do just as well. Narcs crave daily doses of supply. I call it the four A's: admiration, attention, affection, and affirmation. If they don't get it, they can react with a tantrum.

#4 - Feeling embarrassed

This one is kind of ironic, seeing as narcissists take great pleasure in embarrassing, demeaning and humiliating other people. They are renowned for saying things like, 'I was only joking,' or 'You can't take a joke,' or 'Stop being so sensitive,' and expecting others to be on board with their hurtful and derogatory comments. But when others do the same thing to the narc, the response is a tantrum to put most two-year-olds to shame.

Handling the Abuse: 6 Things to Remember to About Narcissism

We all know that narcs are manipulative - so much so, they can fool those closest to them and even therapists and experts. Even when you discover who the narcissist truly is, and what all of their characteristics stand for, they can still manipulate you into thinking you're wrong. They can twist your mind into believing their version of reality, regardless of the evidence stacked against that false reality. In order to combat this mental puppeteering, I want to use this chapter to outline things you should remember when confronting the toxic ways of your spouse. Ideally, I'd like you to keep this information at the forefront of your mind, ready to use it when you need to remind yourself of what's really going on. Then, ultimately, I'd like it to serve as a gateway to you cutting the tether that ties you emotionally to your abuser.

1st Thing to Remember: Narcissists will unmask themselves quicker when they think you're unaware of who they truly are.

Straight-up confrontation of their narcissistic ways will result in even more manipulation and narcissistic rage, which will cause you to stay spinning in the cycle of abuse.

Should you pretend to be the naïve and docile, rather than the wise spouse who knows what the narc is doing, and you'll get yourself an abuser who won't work half as hard to conceal their manipulation, their toxicity and their glee in bringing others down. Their mask will slip faster and more frequently because they don't feel like they have to make such an effort in maintaining their false image around you. They (wrongly) assume that you're gullible enough to believe their front, which satisfies their egotistical needs without them having to go to too much effort.

This also gives you the ability to notice their behavior more deliberately, because it will be less diluted by their attempts to convince you of their false self. By the time the narc has realized that you've caught on to their game, you can be well on your way out of the door. That is why it's preferable that you never refer to the abuser as a 'narcissist'; it will only flare up their rage and cause a backlash from them. Even the strongest of people can buckle and retreat when faced with narcissistic rage.

This rage isn't the only response narcs have to your revelation of the truth. In response to your acknowledgment of their manipulation and narcissism, some will work harder to love-bomb you and idealize you, which makes you more confused and doubtful about your perception about the true nature of their character.

They will do everything they can possibly conjure up to punish you or coerce you into staying with them–including trying to make you remember the good times and manipulating you by using the good memories you have with them. Despite the awfulness and abuse of a narcissistic relationship, there are always good times that have been had (usually at the start of the relationship during the initial love-bombing phase). Narcs use this as an emotionally manipulative way to coax you back to them, hoping that your happy memories will serve as suffice bait to remain in the relationship. At the same time that they're throwing little crumbs of affection and adoration, they're also scheming on how to best use what resources of yours they can get before they discard you for the final time. Even the narc knows the jig is up at this point.

If you prepare your final exit as quietly and secretly as possible (complete with a pre-prepped safety plan), you have a much better chance of leaving safely with your sanity intact. Hopefully, you can leave in a good financial place, but I understand it's not always the case, especially if your other half is the breadwinner or if they know your incomings and outgoings inside out. For this, my advice would be to just get out. You can always find ways to earn more money, to become financially stable - you can never get the time back that you spend in a toxic, abusive, relationship.

The narc may think you're a fool when you first leave. But once they come to realize you had the upper hand all along, they'll be infuriated for completely different reasons–mostly, due to the loss of control and the lack of control that they smugly thought they had.

2nd Thing to Remember: One of their biggest fears that a narcissist has being caught and held accountable for their behavior–so always document their abuse whenever you can.

You can use this knowledge of a manipulator's fear of exposure to your own advantage. Document all incidents of abuse, gaslighting, lying, manipulation and aggression so that you have it on hand should you ever need to take legal action or obtain a restraining order.

Narcissists care very deeply about their social status, what people perceive them as and their reputation, so if they feel they may be exposed as guilty for their crimes, they'll scurry away laughably quickly because they will now see you as a 'high-risk' individual. They're ultra-paranoid about being caught out and exposed–so even just a subtle dropping of a hint that you're onto them (for example, mentioning that you've been talking with someone else about what's been happening–ideally someone they aren't able to manipulate) can cause them to run away.

I believe this is a really great way to protect yourself: writing, bullet pointing or journaling as much as you possibly can give you a secret upper hand the narc knows nothing about. Remember to download your text messages and keep them, or screenshot them and file them somewhere safe. Keep your messages factual, doing your best to avoid emotion, which I know is hard, but it's a must if you want to claw back your power. Emotions and feelings can't be proved, particularly when in court, but facts absolutely can. Note the times and dates of everything where possible.

Although difficult to do, remember that it's important to stay calm whenever reacting to a narc's nastiness, threats, and provocations through texting, calls, e-mails, or any other form of communication. The narcissist is very likely also trying to ensure that they also have you on the record, gathering 'evidence' to show the world and prove you were crazy and psycho all along. They'll pull out this evidence when they're trying to paint you as an unfit parent or an unstable, abusive ex (despite the fact that they're the abusive one). Remember to always appear unaffected and stick to the facts if you need to communicate with them.

If required, photograph injuries or any stalking behavior (if you can), keep voicemails and any posted letters that are threatening. Screenshot everything you possibly can. It can all be useful to you in the future should you ever need to take legal action - it can even serve as a way to go back and understand the reality of what you endured. I know I kept a lot of evidence, screenshots, emails, and threatening letters for a while after my relationship with my abuser ended. I kept them longer than I needed to, simply to ground me, make me realize just how far I'd come, and remind me never, ever to allow myself to endure that kind of abuse again.

3rd Thing to Remember: Your indifference is their Achilles heel.

Are you plotting petty revenge? Mulling over how you can get your abuser back for their emotional torture (when you muster the strength to do so)? Replaying over and over in your head all of the ways you can hurt them as much as they've hurt you?

If you are thinking this was, I wouldn't blame you. I understand it, because it was me for a period of my life, too. But, knowing what I know now, I have to stress that you need to forget any petty revenge that you may be thinking of; narcissists see all of your emotional replies to them (both positive and negative) as ego-buffing attention, and they strive for that. By plotting and exacting revenge, you'll be feeding them their much-needed supply. They'll relish in your attempts to get back at them, knowing that revenge comes from a place of strong emotion. If you have emotion, it means you care. And that's all the narc needs to know to get a kick.

Instead, refocus on you. Cliche as this may sound, I can't stress it enough (remember the phrase, 'the best revenge is success when the need for retribution takes over'). Focus on rebuilding a better life for yourself. It won't be long until you're moving forward, taking back your life and thinking less and less of your abuser.

If you do let them access to your emotional responses, do this in the knowledge that they will use it to feed off of the attention you're giving them, and continue to sap you of your sense of self.

That's why I feel that it's so important to go no contact (or more a case of low contact if you have a child with a narcissist) to stop them from their parasitic ways of feeding off of you and your empathy. Eventually, you won't care what they're up to or who they're doing it with, because you'll know that all they're doing is repeating a very similar cycle of abuse with their newest source of supply. And, laughably ironically, it's utter indifference drives a narc wild.

4th Thing to Remember: They want you back just so they can have the final say.

Narcissists hate (I repeat hate) being discarded because it shows a loss of power and is seen as a huge threat to their perceived superiority. If you were the one who wanted the breakup, it means they didn't have the complete power and control over you that they feel entitled to have in their relationships. They need to have the last word, they need to leave you utterly bereft and they need to be so wanted by you that you crumble without them; they need to feel like you would be unable to move on after being in a relationship with them.

That's why they come crawling back and ask for another chance, time and time again. It's not because they're missing you and feel pain without you. It's because they miss feeling powerful, in control of you and like they own you.

Whenever a narcissist may sense that you are leaving the relationship or becoming distant, they will try their hardest to suck you back in. There's a horrible abusive episode, then a loved-up reconciliation for a short time, then a recurring buildup of tension and intensity, then another inevitable abusive episode. The cycle repeats and repeats. As with many forms of abuse, the rage gets worse each time you reconcile. Every abusive episode gets worse. If you think back to your own experience, have you found that the abuse had gotten worse over time, with the worst episodes getting harder to handle each time?

5th Thing to Remember: You're not inferior to their new spouse or source of supply (read: victim).

It's important to remember that narcissists really don't see their spouses as people-as humans–they see them as mere objects, as their source of supply, their ego-boosting commodity. Supply is like produce; when one supply has dried up, they'll go out and seek another supply.

However, the narc always likes you to think that the reason they've discarded you is that you're more disposable than others, 'less than' the other supplies they can have, or somehow defective so they had to let you go. That's why narcs are renowned for comparing you to their horrible exes or their 'superior' newer spouses (read: targets). In order to not be pulled into this emotionally charged form of crazy-making, recollect how the narc talked about their 'awful' ex at the beginning of your relationship.

This was in the early stages of idealization, and was a way to make you feel for them, to want to show them that people are good, and for you to open up to them. Really, the chances are high that they called their ex-partner 'a psycho' along with a whole other tirade of unflattering words–which is likely how they're going to relay you to their latest source of supply.

No matter what, they always repeat the cycle. To the narcissist, you are no different from their other unsuspecting victims, even if they'd like you to think that you're beneath all of them.

6th Thing to Remember: Pity is a much-used ploy.

Narcissists love to paint a portrait of themselves as very charitable and kind person in the early stages of every relationship they enter. It's one of the things that makes them so compelling, intriguing and seemingly charismatic; not just to you, but to many people around them on the outside. It's what disarms people enough for the narcissist to get away with their deceitful manipulative ways.

Some people truly are kind and selfless, which are such nice traits to see in another being. Narcissists, however, use the image of kindness and humbleness to mask their true nefarious inner self. A narcissist who is contemptuous and sneaky can hide it extremely well during the first stages of a relationship (despite there sometimes being subtle put-downs and so on) but trust that their inherent narcissism will eventually reveal itself.

Another common tactic that narcissists will count on when manipulating you is the use of the pity ploy. Narcs will try to obtain then cling onto your sympathy, leaving you open and emotionally vulnerable to them. If they have your pity, then they have your empathy and compassion - and these wonderful traits are seen as vulnerabilities by an emotional manipulator.

They will present you with a plethora of sob stories and tales of woe right from the beginning of the relationship so you're more likely to see them as poor, misunderstood victims rather than the malicious perpetrator of abuse. Quite often, the narc will offer up a 'lost child' act; they'll be clingy, helpless and a victim of a traumatic past. Whilst elements of their past may have some truth to it (only sometimes; and it's usually exaggerated to make them seem more hard done by), they don't hesitate to feed you what you need to hear to feel upset on their behalf.

Victims and defenseless people connect us to our natural human emotions of compassion, so the narc's false tears and pity ploys really do work - well. If you find yourself feeling a ton of pity for someone who frequently hurts you (or even other people) and who actively campaigns for your sympathy, it's likely that you have a sociopathic narcissist on your hands.

To be a survivor of abuse, you need to be strategic. You can't just hope for it, you need to work towards freeing yourself of the narc's clutches. You need to be able to recognize a manipulator's tales of woe and fake pity stories immediately and be able to resist. This is especially the case if there is no real change in their horrible behavior when you've mentioned it to them.

When you begin to see how put-on their fake remorse really is, you'll find you have a lot less time and sympathy for their excuses for abusive behavior. This will, over time, make you drift farther away from your idealized thinking of your abuser's fabricated world, and bring you closer to carving your path to freedom from the narcissist.

***

That brings this book to a close. Narcissistic rage is still something that's fairly unknown to the survivor community; whilst we've undoubtedly felt the hurtful effects of it, putting a name to the horrible treatments isn't as common.

I hope that you've got a newfound understanding of what rage is, and know that being on the receiving end isn't a reflection on you - it's everything to do with the narcissist.

Here's to healing.

Don't miss out!

Visit the website below and you can sign up to receive emails whenever Lauren Kozlowski publishes a new book. There's no charge and no obligation.

https://books2read.com/r/B-A-PTHI-BRXBB

BOOKS 2 READ

Connecting independent readers to independent writers.

Also by Lauren Kozlowski

Red Flags: The Dating Red Flag Checklist to Spot a Narcissist, Abuser or Manipulator Before They Hurt You
Narcissistic Ex
Malignant Narcissism: Understanding and Overcoming Malignant Narcissistic Abuse
What a Narcissist Does at the End of a Relationship: Dealing With and Understanding the Aftermath of a Narcissistic Relationship
Narcissistic Rage: Understanding & Coping With Narcissistic Rage, Silent Treatment & Gaslighting
How to go No Contact With a Narcissist
Trauma Bonding: Understanding and Overcoming the Traumatic Bond in a Narcissistic Relationship
Coercive Control: Breaking Free From Psychological Abuse
Narcissistic Stalker

Lightning Source UK Ltd.
Milton Keynes UK
UKHW020303041022
409859UK00008B/1671